LOVE LUCY

LOVE LUCY

DIANE JOHNSON

J. Merrill
PUBLISHING

J Merrill Publishing, Inc., Columbus 43207
www.JMerrill.pub

Library of Congress Control Number: 2021904427
ISBN-13: 978-1-950719-94-5 (Paperback)
ISBN-13: 978-1-950719-93-8 (eBook)

Title: Love Lucy
Author: Diane Johnson

CONTENTS

FOREWORD

My mother's name is Lucy Mae Johnson, and I had the distinct pleasure of her friendship and kinship for over 50 years. She was always after me to help write her story; it was something she talked about constantly. I should have helped her, but I was always so busy.

During recuperation from surgery some years back, I did take the time to write down my mother's life recollections. I will always cherish the time we had sitting at the kitchen table; she is sipping on her decaf coffee and me a hot cup of tea as she shared her life story with me. I count it a joy and a privilege to be able to finally fulfill the promise I made to tell my mother's story.

Beginning with my mother's memoirs in her voice and ending with my recollections of the life-changing and spiritually affirming moments of our time together. My only regret is that she did not get a chance to read the book.

By sharing her story, I feel that her dream is fulfilled, even if it posthumously.

So, grab a cup of coffee, or whatever pleases your palette, and enjoy the book that my mother so longed for.

1

SWEET LUCY'S STORY

My great-grandmother shared many recollections about slavery. She told me about not having shoes to wear because they feared slaves with shoes would be more likely to run away. In Columbia County in the northwest portion of Florida, where the staple crops included peanuts, cotton, and tobacco, my family's story began. Many plantation owners made a substantial living raising tobacco and owning slaves. My great-grandmother was about 9 years old when Abraham Lincoln was elected as the 16th president of the United States, and 11 when he signed the Emancipation Proclamation.

She was married to a man by the name of Henry McNish at a very young age. Henry came from the

McNish plantation. It was one of the largest plantations in the area. To this day, there are many African Americans with the surname of McNish residing in Columbia County.

My great grandfather Henry had 40 acres of land that he probably received from a land grant after the civil war. He and Lucy Anne began to farm and raise a family. They were blessed with 11 children, three boys, and eight girls. The boys' names were Frazey, William, and George; the girls were Charlotte, Harriet, Ethel, Priscilla, Cora, Posthene, Polly Anne, and Ruth. My great grandfather was one of the few black men who owned land. His farm was beautiful and stood out from among the rest. There was a beautiful orchard filled with plum and peach trees. They also raised cows, hogs, horses, and chickens. Most of the work was done by the family and required long hours and dedication to make the farm one of the best in the county. My great grandfather was an inspiration to blacks in the community. His wife was a great help to him in developing the land; she was also the mid-wife and lay doctor for many local residents. She healed many with her home remedies and tonics.

Once, there was a family that called for her when their child was deathly ill with pneumonia. Lucy Anne took a pipe stem and inserted it into the child's nostril, and sucked out the phlegm, which cleared his airway restoring his breathing. Henry and Lucy Anne instilled faith in God, moral integrity, and hard work into their children. Henry continued to encourage the black community to be responsible for their own affairs and not trust their land deeds to anyone. This raised the rile of certain unscrupulous men who sought to perpetuate intimidation and fear to keep the black farmers under subjection.

Henry told his wife about his feelings of dark foreboding concerning the threats against his life. He admonished her to be strong and keep the land no matter what happened to him. He made the land their property to be willed to his wife and children unto the 3rd generation upon his death.

My great grandfather had good reason to feel a sense of pending terror. When Henry was talking with some other men in town as they stood on the local grocer's stoop, a shot rang out one midsummer morning.

When the dust cleared, they say it was Henry who fell to the ground. Mr. Otis, one of the local white farmers, was sick of what he called Henry's rebellious talk and decided to put an end to it before all the black farmers were out of control.

Mr. Otis shot Henry in the back in broad open daylight, and no one laid a hand on him. The family was in shock and grief-stricken as their beloved husband and father lay dead on the ground for hours as they waited all day for the authorities to come and investigate the shooting.

One day My Aunt Annie Mae shared her recollection of the tragic event with me. She recalled the body of her grandpa lying on the ground in the blistering hot Florida sun as they all huddled together in fear and grief.

Aunt Annie Mae said that white foam was coming from her Grandpa's mouth. My mother, who was no more than 5, remembered the grief and feeling of helplessness that her grandfather's death brought to the family. It was told that no formal charges were brought against Mr. Otis. In fact, many could breathe a sigh of relief that the troublesome Henry was dead.

Lucy Anne remembered her husband's instructions about keeping the farm together. She was a strong woman but could do nothing against the fear that overshadowed her sons. William left town with a group of white men promising him work in Miami. He promised to send money home to help the family.

Weeks turned into months with no word from William. Lucy Anne feared the worst had happened to her son. Lucy Anne tried for months to find William to no avail; he was never heard from again. Frazey, the second son, made his escape to New York City, where he found work and began a new life in the north. It wasn't long before Lucy, Anne received word that she had lost yet another son. Frazey perished in a house fire, and because of the distance, Lucy Anne was unable to retrieve his remains or take care of his affairs.

Frazey had a bank account with his sister Ethel's name on it. But because the family was too poor to travel, it was lost because the bank insisted the only way to receive the funds from the account had to be done in person.

George, Lucy Anne's youngest son, also died with very little detail concerning his death. There were rumors that he met his father Henry's same fate. The women of the family remained a very tight-knit group. Charlotte, Ethel, and Cora remained with Lucy Anne on the farm. They worked tirelessly to keep things running but could barely afford to pay the property tax. Each year at tax time, to seize the property, one white farmer would pay the taxes and insist Lucy Anne vacate the farm. My mother remembers an occasion when an old white man came to their house and threatened to bum the house down if they did not leave. As my great-grandmother was affectionately called, Grandma Doty just calmly kept rocking in her chair and slowly puffed her pipe. She told the men that if they burned the house down, they would have to bum it down with her in it cause she wasn't going anywhere.

Lucy Anne did the best she could to keep the farm, but without any men to help, the farm soon began to deteriorate. Gone was the beautiful plum orchard and peach trees. The horses, cows, and chickens were sold to provide money and food. A portion of the land was leased out to other farmers.

Lucy Anne never lacked for company. Her daughter Ethel never married and stayed on with her mother working to help support the household. Cora, my grandmother, married a man by the name of Tom Seymour, and they had 3 children, Henry, Beatrice, and Gladys. The marriage was short-lived, and Cora soon returned with her children to live with Lucy Anne. Her sister Charlotte married and built an addition to her mother's house where she and her husband lived.

My mother Beatrice was Cora's eldest daughter and was known for her beauty and free spirit. She was a beautiful woman with smooth, clear skin, the color of honey. Her eyes were soft and brown, and her hair was black and always immaculately coiffed. As she was affectionately called, Bea was the proverbial good time girl; she loved music and dancing. She was entertaining and loved to be entertained. Her marriage to my father Milton Williams was her second.

They had three children, Lula Pearl, Solomon, and me, Lucy Mae. My brother Anthony was from my mother's first marriage and was raised by his father's people. Just like her mother Cora, my mother's marriage did not last very long. Beatrice desired to get away from the farm and see the world, so when marriage offered her a chance at a better life, she gladly accepted.

Mr. Roosevelt King was struck by her beauty and fun-loving spirit, but he soon discovered Beatrice did not trade in her dancing shoes for an apron.

Her first marriage was brief, just long enough to produce my brother Anthony. Beatrice left her first-born child in the care of his father's relatives. This left her to pursue her free-spirited lifestyle. She eventually left the farm life of Columbia county. She ventured to Lakeland, Florida a small, but modest town some three hours away but a far cry from the drudgery of the country life.

2

LITTLE BIG EYE LUCY

I was born in Lakeland, Florida, on August 2, 1936; I actually celebrated August 1 because I was born very early in the morning. Everybody just considered it was still the 1st. My mother named me after my great grandmother Lucy Anne. I never felt myself a very attractive child, not like my beautiful mother or my sister Lula Pearl. She had long, thick black hair and seemed to be everybody's favorite. I had short, thin hair and large wide eyes that betrayed my deepest thoughts. My eyes were a constant source of ridicule from other children. They taunted me with names like "Big-eyed Lucy." I wore a mask of insecurity while hiding the hurt I felt inside.

My youngest brother Solomon was born on August 10, 1938. He was never called Solomon but went by the name Leroy. He never knew his name was Solomon until he was an adult and required a copy of his birth certificate.

My brother Leroy was given to my mother's aunt Priscilla, whom we all called Aunt Tug. Aunt Tug was married and lived in Lakeland; she had one child, a boy who died tragically in a swimming accident. My mother felt he would get good care in the hands of Aunt Tug. Leroy seemed to be reasonably happy. We did not get a chance to see him much, only when Aunt Tug came to visit. With my brother gone, my mother soon carried my sister and I back to the farm to live with my grandmother and great-grandmother; the area later became known as Scrub Town. I was around 6 years old when my mother left us with my grandmother Cora and great-grandmother Lucy Anne. Life on the farm left little time for play. Even as young children, we were required to clean the fireplace, retrieve wood, and kindle and make sure the fire was started first thing in the morning. There was no water supply, so water had to be hauled from a neighboring farm at least 10 miles away.

Clothes had to be washed at the wash pond, a pond where everybody washed their clothes.

There was an enormous black kettle with a fire underneath where you put your clothes and let them soak in the boiling hot water. The clothes were hung nearby in the sun to dry. The wash pond seemed to be miles away; at least, it seemed that way to me as a child of just six years old. To my surprise, my mother returned after a year or so and took my sister and I back to Lakeland. I can remember going to school and enjoying it so

much. My second-grade teacher was named Miss Walker, a slim, neat woman who treated the children kind and stimulated my interest in learning.

I was a very eager student and read books every chance I could. I purposed in my mind that one day I would be a teacher just like Miss Walker. My sister Lula Pearl was also very smart. She had a quiet demeanor, and I was vocal and strong-willed like my great grandmother Lucy Anne.

We lived in a house that belonged to my Aunt Ruth, who married Richard Gordon. They worked on the orange grove. Aunt Ruth worked as a domestic, and Uncle Richard was the caretaker.

They stayed all week on the orange grove and came back to town on Friday night. When Aunt Ruth and Uncle Richard came home, we could look forward to sumptuous meals, dancing, music, and merriment. My mother would leave us with Aunt Ruth every weekend, and during the week, she would slip out when she thought we were fast asleep.

3

BACK TO THE FARM

It wasn't long before my sister, and I went back to the farm. I can't remember how we got there or why we left, but I do remember the sadness of having to return to the drudgery of farm life. I withdrew into a shell and regressed academically. I went from a bright, intelligent child to a wide-eyed, forsaken little girl. I imagined how the young slaves must have felt as they worked and worked and worked, with never any time to play and enjoy the wonders of childhood.

At a young age, I was hired to work in the homes of white families to wash dishes and oftentimes babysit for children my own age. I never saw any money, because it was always given to my grandmother Cora. I can remember telling one of the people I worked for not to give my money to Grandma Cora but to Grandma Lucy Anne.

I told them that my grandmother would only take my money and get drunk. My words must have gotten back to my grandmother because I felt she never could quite show me the affection she showed for my sister. My mother's sister, Gladys, had one child, a girl whom she named Ethel after her aunt. Like my brother Leroy, no one ever called her Ethel; she was always known as Lois. Gladys died when Lois was just two years old. Gladys was unmarried, so Lois was sent to live with Grandma Cora.

My grandmother treated Lois with sympathetic kindness, as did everyone who came in contact with her. Everyone felt compassion for the little girl without a mother or father. It was rumored that when Gladys went to take care of my mother Beatrice during childbirth, my father, Milton, took advantage of young Gladys and became pregnant. Before my father died, he admitted to me that my cousin Lois was also his child. Before I knew Lois was my sister, I always loved her as a sister.

4

BACK TO THE CITY

I had an unexpected reprieve from the farm. When I was about 9 years old, my brother Leroy and I were out in the woods gathering kindling and wood. We came across a small tree stump that had dried up and would make excellent firewood. The stump would require some pressure to fully remove it from the ground. I told my brother, who was about seven at the time, to strike the stump while I held it steady.

My brother's striking iron was about 1" thick, 2" wide, and about 18' inches long. I was holding the tree stump and planned to move my hand as he hit it. My brother came down on the stump with all of his might. In fact, just before striking, he warned me to move my hand. The striking iron caught the ring finger of my left hand.

Blood squirted everywhere as I screamed in pain. My brother and I had to run at least a mile to get home. My great aunt Charlotte doused my finger in turpentine, gathered some spider web, and wrapped it around my dangling finger. Someone ran to Mr. Theo's house. He was a white farmer that lived about 2 miles away.

Mr. Theo came to take us into town in his truck; he let Aunt Charlotte and me ride in the cab with him. High Springs was the nearest town, and it was an agonizing five miles away. When we got to town, we went to Doctor Week's office. He was the only doctor, and black people had to go to the back entrance. The nurse removed the dressing that my aunt had put on my finger, held my hand over the sink, and picked out the bone fragments. Dr. Weeks stitched my dangling finger back into place as I screamed out in sheer agony.

When I grew older, I was often ashamed of my misshapen finger, not realizing it was a miracle that my finger was saved. Because I would require additional medical care, my grandmother sent for my mother to come to get me to have close access to the doctor. This was the first time I was alone with my mother.

Things had changed for her; she no longer lived in Aunt Ruth's house but had a small room in a boarding house right above the town picture show. Unfortunately, she had not changed her ways. I was left alone and neglected. In fact, my finger went unattended, and the stitches stayed in way too long.

5

MOTHER ROBINSON SENT FROM GOD

Everyone called the lady that ran the rooming house, Mother Robinson. Mother Robinson was a pastor of a small church. She and her members were referred to as sanctified folks. They believed in receiving the Holy Ghost and speaking in tongues, and dancing in the Spirit. Mother Robinson had compassion on me and would often take me with her to church service. I was enthralled by the excitement, music, dancing, and clapping. Mother Robinson and her members prayed for me and showed such love and kindness. Mother Robinson's prayer and kindness for a young waif buoyed me through a most difficult and impoverished childhood. I believe she was sent from God to prepare the way for a great calling that was placed on my life.

6

BACK TO THE FARM AGAIN

My father had a brother named Clemmie, who lived in town with his wife, Gussie. They did not have any children and took an interest in me. My mother gladly allowed them to keep me along as they wanted. My uncle was not a very loving man. Still, he did show appreciation for my ability to cook, clean, and take care of myself. He wanted to legally adopt me, and of course, my mother consented. My father, on the other hand, was against it. I guess my father felt the least he could do was to ensure we all stayed together. My father exerted his parental rights and took me from my Uncle Clemmie and Aunt Gussie, and drove over three hours to deliver me back to my grandmother.

The three-hour drive was about the longest time I could remember spending with my father. I don't remember much conversation, just the loud hum of the car's engine. My father delivered me safe and sound back to the hands of my grandmother Cora. I had mixed emotions about my return. I was happy to see my sister. However, I realized all the hard work that lay before me. There was no electricity or running water, two conveniences that I had grown accustomed to in the city. Despite it all, there were still some fond memories associated with living with my grandmother.

As I remember, it was the simple things, like the time after they would butcher a hog. First, they would clean it with boiling hot water. We had a smokehouse that we stored the meat, but there was so much that came from the hog. There was the crackling made from the fat, lard, intestine to stuff the sausage, liver pudding, hog head cheese, just to name a few. Hog killing time was one of those occasions where it required adult labor. That left the children to run and play and sneak some crackling every now and then. Hog butchering was a collective effort; usually, families got together and made it into a social gathering. We got a chance to see cousins and friends we had not seen in months. I can't emphasize enough how much the occasion lent itself to a time for a child to run and play and not think about chores.

Another fond memory is that of my grandmother making homemade butter and buttermilk. They had what they called clabber milk, which consisted of milk left out a few days, and then sugar was added to it. We would eat it or mix it with biscuit dough to produce the best biscuits in the world. My grandmother's sister, whom we called Aunt Posthene, was married to a man named Ernest. They collaborated with my great aunt Charlotte's moonshine business by running a little nightclub that most people in Scrub town called a Juke.

I guess they called them that because the music usually came from a jukebox. However, my aunt's Juke's music was not from a jukebox but was performed live by Uncle Ernest. In my opinion, he played the guitar more soulful than BB King. I had a good head for numbers, and they had me count and keep track of the money.

I enjoyed watching the grownups dance and listening to my uncle Ernest's sweet sound on the guitar. Uncle Ernest would play his guitar until he saw my great aunt Posthene dancing or talking to another man. The music would stop, and he would grab my aunt and crack her over the head with his guitar. I felt sorry for my aunt and couldn't imagine how a man that could play such sweet music could be so mean.

At about the age of 11 or 12, my sister and I decided to run away and join the other migrant workers and go to pick whatever crop was in season. Now that I think back, I wonder how two young girls could do such a thing and know how to take care of themselves. Somehow my grandmother got wind of our location and sent word to send us back to Scrub town. Thus, ended our adventurous escape.

My sister Lula Pearl ended up pregnant at a very early age. I took on the responsibility of being an aunt with passion and dedication to my little nephew named Thomas Lee. We affectionately called him, Tom-a-Lee. There was some question concerning my nephew's paternity. But because my sister had been seeing a boy by the name of Tom Payne, we naturally assumed that he was the father; however, many years later, it was discovered my sister had been mistaken about her first child's paternity. I stuck around for a while to help my sister take care of the baby, and even my grandmother would comment on how well I took care of my nephew; she often said that the child should have been mine.

7

FAREWELL TO BEAUTIFUL BEATRICE

When I was about 16, I ventured out on my own and lived in a little town called Perrine, Florida. I received word that my mother Beatrice had passed away. Beatrice had a small insurance policy that made me the beneficiary. I often wondered why my mother chose me as the beneficiary; however, I later understood that I was the one that the spirit of responsibility fell. She knew that I would take care of business and ensure everything was taken care of. I was more like my great grandmother Lucy Anne the pipe-smoking, no joking medicine woman. I think back about my mother Bea and how she would want me to come and care for her while she was sick. She had a stroke and was partially paralyzed at 35 and passed away when she was 39.

I remember how much my mother loved to put so much salt on her food; no one could ever eat behind her because it was very salty. When she got sick, she would want me to come and lay in the bed with her until she fell asleep. I was ashamed to admit that I was scared and would lie next to her with my feet dangling off the bed. I was scared because the word was that someone had worked roots on my mother; that's why she was afflicted. I know now that she probably had high blood pressure due to all the salt she ate. The funny thing is, although my mother suffered a stroke, she still managed to attract men and had a boyfriend until the day she passed.

8

ANOTHER ENCOUNTER
WITH GOD

While living in Perrine, Florida, I met a wonderful family, all of them filled with the spirit of God, dedicated to the church, and serving the Lord. Since the time I was a little girl and had the chance to meet with Mother Robinson, I was attracted to being a woman of God. The Ingram family I befriended in Perrine was originally from somewhere in the Caribbean. The father and mother spoke with an accent, and the father was the pastor of the church I attended. The Ingram family was like my second family, and I was blessed to catch Bill Ingram's eye, one of the Ingram children. He asked me to marry him when I was just 17 years old. To get married, I had to travel back home to Lakeland to obtain my birth certificate.

When I arrived in Lakeland, I ran into my cousin Lois. Lois introduced me to a tall, dark, handsome young man from Sparta, Georgia, named Willie Johnson. Willie had begged my cousin to introduce him to me as he saw us walking up the Boulevard and couldn't take his eyes off me. I never thought I was the attractive sort of woman. But I did have a figure like a Coca-Cola bottle that I inherited from my mother, Beatrice.

As fate would have it, I never returned to Perrine and broke Bill Ingram's heart by abandoning him for tall, dark, and handsome Willie. I married Willie Johnson after seven months of courting. My father's wife, whom I affectionately referred to as Miss Rosa, pulled me to the side and told me not to marry Willie because I would be making a big mistake. Who knew that her prophecy would come true? I married Willie regardless, without the benefit of even a wedding ring. I spent my wedding night in the rooming house where he was staying all by myself. Willie was out acting like a single man on our first night of marriage.

9

BIRTH OF A FAMILY

I always stayed true to my spiritual roots and sought a church to join and found one pastored by Bishop Henry Ross. The church was of the apostolic denomination. The women were modestly dressed, covered their heads with prayer scarves or hats, and wore no make-up, pants, or sleeveless dresses. My husband never found that very attractive and sought out more worldly women to spend time with.

Willie joined the army shortly after we were married, and I followed him to Fort Benning, Georgia, where our first child was born. Donald Wayne Johnson was born on September 6, 1957. I was happy beyond belief, and with all my might, I mothered him in every way possible.

Willie completed his tour of duty in the army; was honorably discharged. We returned to Lakeland, Florida, where our second child Diane Lorane Johnson was born June 20, 1959. I wanted to name her Mary, but Willie did not like the name and named her after one of the hospital nurses. He misspelled the middle name, and Diane was stuck with Lorane instead of Lorraine as a middle name. Like most blacks in the south during the late fifties early sixties, the lure to go north for better jobs and opportunities was ever-present. Willie's father had settled in Columbus, Ohio, so he felt it was a good chance to find better work up north. Willie was always aspiring to improve himself. He took coursework to complete his high school diploma. He was doing pretty good working for an exterminator, but the call to do more always compelled him to seek greater things. I was satisfied with my children and the church and had no desire to move away from family and friends.

Willie left for Ohio in 1959 and promised to send for me to join him when he found work. My daughter Diane was 9 months old when we finally got the funds to join him in Columbus, Ohio. Little did I know my life would never be the same again. Things would be cold and harsh as the Ohio winter. Willie was staying in a rooming house, and the landlady did not allow children or sleepover guests. I had no idea what I was getting into. I should have known things would be rough when I arrived with two small kids, one with a wet diaper and no one at the bus station to pick us up.

I caught a cab to the address my husband gave me, and again no one was there to welcome us. I sat in the hallway with the tired and hungry children until a kind man saw us and invited us into his room to wait.

Willie's father was Mr. Bill Johnson, and he had an old, dilapidated rental house that he let us stay in. The wind passed right through the walls so much that I called them breathing walls, and the rats were so big the kids thought they were cats.

In 1961 we were blessed with another child that Willie named Willie David Johnson Jr. He came into the world weighing nearly 11 pounds. He was the biggest baby they had seen in the hospital in a long time.

Life was tough, but I had the best blessing I could have ever hoped for... my children. I loved them so and loved just looking at them and caring for them. Although Willie and I did not have the ideal marriage, I had the children I so longed for.

My husband went through several jobs. Initially, he tried construction work with his father. But he had such sensitive skin that broke out, making it impossible to do the work. He tried selling insurance but could not manage to keep the customers' policy money separate from his own. Finally, he found a civil service position at the Defense Construction Supply Center.

We found a place on the Southside of the city called Lincoln Park. It was a government-sponsored housing project set aside for low-income tenants. Coming from the breathing walls and rat trap we were staying in; Lincoln Park was a dream come true. In 1967 the Lord blessed me once again with another son that Willie named Timothy Jonathan Johnson. He was a beauty like his grandmother Beatrice.

When Tim was born, I went to work for North American Rockwell. I was trained to solder the circuit boards for the aircraft. I missed being home with the kids, but the money would help the family move out of the projects. The problem with me working was the more I worked, the less Willie contributed to the household, and I ended up bearing a lot of the household expenses.

It came a time that I saw I could make it alone and was determined to leave Willie and go my separate way. I filed for divorce, but the judge would not grant it because I was pregnant. I guess there was a legal standard about delaying divorce hearings until after childbirth.

Willie was determined not to divorce and worked with me to find a house. I had always dreamed of owning a house. The house we found was in a brand new development on the south side of the city

called Southfield, and it was just beautiful; three bedrooms, split level, large back yard everything I dreamed of. A lot of living went into that house, and the Lord blessed me to raise my children and love them with all my heart. Not bad for a little big-eyed farm girl name Lucy Mae.

10

A DAUGHTER'S EYE VIEW

I feel such a sense of joy having documented my mother's memoirs. However, I would be remiss to end this book without my recollections as her only daughter and amour bearer. These memories of mine are of my mother and the greatest friendship that life could afford. I rebelled like any teenager, but it never lasted long. I remember one year for my mother's birthday, I used my allowance and bought her a big oversized card that had a picture of a Chinese lady dressed in a traditional kimono with a huge fan in her hand. The inside of the card read, "from your number one fan, happy birthday." Whenever I got mad, or my mother disciplined me, I would go into her top right dresser drawer and take my card back.

My mother never gave up on me and probably realized that I would eventually mature enough to know she only had my best interest at heart. Certainly, this was true, and I often think of that card and fondly reflect on her patience with me. I know now that she was my number one fan, never wavering in her support, prayer, and love for me. I truly miss her and often chuckle about the "number one fan" card and how true friendship is a blessing no matter where it is found. It is something to be treasured and will result in a beautiful memory as long as you live.

11

FRIENDS FROM THE START

When I was three years old, my mother told me she and my father were in a heated argument about her inability to get her hair done to look presentable. She said; I sat there listening intently as my father said he bought her some hair grease, and that should be enough. Mother said I placed one hand on my hip and the other hand I pointed a finger at him and said, " Is that all? I would not have you ". Thus began a friendship that would last over 50 years. For as long as I can remember, I loved my mother. I always wanted her to be happy, and I knew early on that her marriage was not happy. But she was oh so happy being a mother and poured all her love into her children. We shared a special bond. Being the only daughter became a witness to her struggle to raise a family with an abusive husband. My father was not so much physically abusive as he was psychologically and verbally. He did not make her feel good about herself. He was constantly using language that eroded her self-esteem. I felt it was my mission to stay near to her and help her to be happy.

12

THE WOUNDED CHILD

When I was five years old or so, I overheard my mother talking about not having any money. As I said, I felt my role was to make her life better, so I told her that I knew where she could get some money. As a child, I thought that would make her happy. Well, it did not, and my mother was quite interested in this mysterious source of money that I could lay my hands on. She questioned me about the source of the money. With my overactive imagination, I fabricated a story about a man who had a lot of money.

Before I knew it, my mother had me in the car, and we were riding around the neighborhood trying to figure out where the money man lived. Not only did we ride around until I pointed out some unsuspecting stranger as the culprit, but I was taken to the hospital where I was further interrogated about the money man. I had to endure some testing to determine if I had been molested. The Lord knows I only wanted to make my mother feel better about her lack of money, and here I added to her distress.

I never understood until years later why my mother reacted so strongly about the money man incident. She shared a tragic story of how her grandmother Cora delivered her into the hands of a stranger. She went on to explain that the stranger molested her.

I did not understand how her grandmother could allow a man to just snatch her away. As a young girl, I am sure she did not understand how and why her grandmother, whom she trusted, could allow a stranger to take and violate her. How incredibly sad I was for the wounded little girl in her as she recalled the memory of rape and abuse; then I understood why she was so protective of me.

13

SPECIAL CALL OF GOD

As far back as I can remember, we went to church. The church was located on the east side of the city and was named Rehoboth Temple Church of Christ. I always thought Rehoboth was an odd name for a church, but the name in Hebrew means "room enough." It was spiritual warfare in the Johnson house. For some reason, my dad did not want us to go to church. I have this memory of capitalizing on that fact. Mind you, church was long, and as a child, we had to sit still and be on our best behavior during the course of the long service. After I figured out that Dad was somewhat opposed to our constant church going, I would rouse the devil in him. Mother would quietly get us prepared for church as my father slept off his weekend hangover. Then we would generally slip out of the house without waking him. On one occasion, I really did not want to go to church, so I slipped into their bedroom while my mother was busy with my baby brother. I woke my father and asked him to button my dress so he would know that we were preparing to go to church. I remember him running barefoot in the street, trying to catch up with us to stop my mother from going to church. I really felt awful about my role in the whole thing and never did that again.

14

MIRACLE MOM

I can recall so many miraculous things that happened due to my mother's faith in God. The biggest one was staying with my father for 49 years and making our home and childhood warm and loving. My mother had other children outside of the children she had with my father. Shirley, Nicky, Renee, Jussetta, Lisa, and so many others called her mother. Shirley and Nicky came into our lives when they walked into the church one day looking for help. Mother befriended them and thus began a lifelong connection. I remember following my mother over to Shirley's house to deliver clothes and food. When we got there, the house was full of people hanging out getting high. For one, I wanted to turn and walk out, but I knew my mother would face the challenge head-on. She went from room to room praying and speaking in tongue with me not far behind her. I felt safe following behind my mother. Not long after she had stopped praying, the whole house was strangely quiet, and only Shirley and her daughter remained. My mother was always there to talk Shirley off the ledge as she battled addiction. She became a grandmother to little Nicky. Sometimes, I felt a little jealous about sharing my mother so much but learned that feeling jealous was fruitless because sharing was something I had to get used to.

Renee had lost custody of her kids due to her drug addiction and one day met Mother Johnson when she walked into the church looking for help. She walked directly into a lifelong friendship with my mother. It would take quite a while to recount the nights and days my mother spent counseling and providing spiritual and other resources. I believe God placed me by her side to be the help she needed. Although we were constant companions and thick as thieves, I was the administrative arm that organized the many ways that help was needed. For example, one day, Renee called from jail begging for help. I knew my mother's heart, and all she cared about was helping the souls that

God sent her way. As soon as she told me of the condition, I would figure out how we could get it done. You could say she did the praying, counseling, and teaching while I stood close to ensure she had the resources to get things done.

Mom met Lisa in the neighborhood; she was a divorced mother of 5 children. Lisa was a hard-working woman trying to do the best she could with the kids. She and her husband divorced due to his drug use and inability to help her with the kids.

During her friendship with my mother, we took her in like all the others sharing time, listening, and doing what was needed. Lisa was a good-looking woman and eventually met another man. My mother was a staunch believer in honoring original marriage vows and felt that Lisa should seek to be reconciled with her first husband and not seek another relationship. Lisa did not listen to my mother's advice and eventually remarried. After months of trying, Lisa and her new husband were anxiously awaiting the birth of a new baby. Lisa asked my mother to go with her to the hospital when she went into labor. The birth proved difficult, and after many hours of labor, the doctor told Lisa they would have to do a c-section.

As they prepared for the procedure, my mother laid her hands on Lisa's stomach. She prayed while she was praying, the baby moved. When the doctor came back to examine Lisa, the baby had moved into the correct birthing position, to his great surprise. Lisa was able to deliver the child without a c-section.

15

MOTHER HERO

I must tell you when I was about eleven, I wanted to hold a carnival for muscular dystrophy. Back then, Jerry Lewis headed the muscular dystrophy charity campaign, and kids could hold backyard carnivals to help raise money. In my packet held all of the things you could do to hold a carnival for charity, including contacting local stores for contributions. I called several stores and was able to get a gift certificate from a store called "Big Bear" and one from "Children's Palace. Everything went well when I picked up the Big Bear certificate, and I used it to buy prizes for the carnival. My dad drove me to Children's Palace; it was a toy store located about 15 minutes from our house. When I went into the store to pick up the gift certificate, the store manager saw me; he said there was no such arrangement made and that I must be mistaken. I left the store in tears. When I told my dad about it, he did nothing but drive me home. I ran into the house and told my mother, who was in the middle of cooking, what happened at the Children's Palace. Before I knew it, she and I were on our way back to the store. I cannot remember exactly what my mother said to the store manager. But I do remember receiving three nice board games to use as carnival prizes. I rode home in awe of her; she was my hero.

In my third year of college, I ran into a young man I thought was the one for me. He was one of the leaders of the largest fraternity on campus, and I thought he was something special. When I decided to join a sorority just so I could be in the Greek circle and maybe have a chance with my crush. I called home for money to join the sorority; mom immediately said "No" because she had a bad feeling about me joining this sorority. Having no success with mom, I decided to try my luck with dad. Lo and behold, my old man came through with the money. I joined the sorority, and yes, I was able to find true love with the fraternity leader.

When I found out I was pregnant and told absolutely no one, not my mother, not my best friend, nobody knew but me. I continued all my activities, and because I had extreme nausea, I actually lost weight. My mother called one day to check on me, and during our conversation, she wanted to share a dream she had. Sharing dreams was nothing unusual because my mother always had dreams. She told me she had a dream about me this time and that I was three months pregnant in the dream. I nearly dropped the phone. I was exactly three months pregnant and had told no one.

My parents wanted to meet my boyfriend and discuss his intentions. Deep down, I knew it was an exercise in futility. The thing I will never forget is my mother looking around my boyfriend's house. She spied my TV in the living room. Now granted, my TV was a small black and white K-Mart special, but it did not matter to mom it was mine. In the awkward silence that permeated the setting, my mother proclaimed loudly, "Diane is that your TV?" I confirmed that it was. She quietly unplugged it, wrapped the cord, and instructed my dad to carry it to the car. She knew that she would become the partner that I needed to raise my son. My mother and I were the perfect teams. Believe it or not, I thought I would be able to have my baby and go back to Central State and complete my education. My mother quickly dashed that dream when she told me that my days staying in the dorm were over. It was a hard pill to swallow, but she pledged to support me all the way and support me she did.

She guided me to the Ohio State University immediately upon my arrival back home. It was all a blur, but somehow with her holding my hand, I registered at OSU spring quarter 1979 and gave birth to a bouncing baby boy summer of 1980.

Fall quarter of 1980, I was back in class at the Ohio State University. My mother made the ultimate sacrifice to support me and encourage me not to give up on my dream. She made sure I had a balance of motherhood and student time. When I needed extra time, she was there. When I needed sleep, she quietly got up at night with the baby. It was seamless the way she provided exactly what I needed.

My close relationship with my mother eventually led me to a relationship with Jesus Christ as well. I knew Jesus could save me because I knew he saved my mother and made her the beautiful woman that she was. I wanted that beauty, that spiritual strength, to be a mother like her.

16

THE PIE LADY

Mother was known as the pie lady. When anybody lost a family member or was going through some adversity, she would bake them one of her delicious pies. There was some type of anointing on her pies because when we walked in with the pies, sad eyes would turn from crying into laughter. God really ministered to people through her kitchen. Mother Lucy was a wonderful cook. Like many women from her generation, the recipes were engraved in her heart and in her mind. As her faithful sidekick and sous chef, I spent many hours doing the prep work. One day my niece Kori expressed an interest in cooking and wanted to learn how to make her grandmother's famous sweet potato pie. We did what we could to record the ingredients of both the pie and the homemade crust recipe. I am so glad we did. Whenever I get to missing mom, I get in the kitchen and make a sweet potato pie. According to my family, you cannot tell the difference between her pies and mine. I have even continued with her tradition of blessing the broken-hearted with a homemade pie fresh out of the oven. I love the smell as the pie bakes in the oven. I embrace the warm memory of me and my mother in the kitchen.

17

I LOVE LUCY

For her 80th birthday, I thought we would have a big celebration with a party and food the whole nine yards. When I asked my mother for her opinion, she preferred to do something on a smaller scale. That was her personality, so unassuming, never too much fuss or big to do for her. So I planned a small intimate affair at my house that included a few friends and family just like she wanted. We decided to make it a brunch to start at 11:00 a.m. on Sunday, August 1, 2016. The menu consisted of a breakfast casserole made of hash browns, eggs, sausage, and cheeses, all baked together to create a delectable casserole. We also had bacon, watermelon, and my mother's homemade biscuits. She made herself because nobody could make biscuits like her.

The attendees included family friends Charlie Knapper and his wife Freda, Tammy Smith, and her sister, Tracy. Family members included my nieces Kori, Kameron, and their sister Khyle, my father and brother Timothy, and brother David called in from San Antonio, Texas.

Happiness was all around that day as Freda, with her anointed voice, serenaded my mother with several of her favorite hymns. There was not a dry eye as everyone honored her with a personal account of how she blessed them. At the end of the day, my mother told everyone it was the best birthday she ever had.

On Monday, November 7, 2016, just over 90 days after her beautiful birthday celebration, my dear friend, comrade, and soul mate stepped from this life to life eternal. We had no warning that it would be her last day. My brother Tim decided to stop at mother's after a dental appointment, and I was there raiding the fridge of any leftovers. It was a fitting end to a great friendship; sharing a meal, then departing with our typical hug and bidding each other a fond adieu with love. As long as I live, I am determined to build upon the foundation that she left. My mother was always kind and caring and had a smile on her face even during the toughest times. Most people think I look a lot like my father until they see me smile. When I smile, you can see my mother's beautiful face and loving spirit in me.

This book is a tribute to her life and a daughter's promise fulfilled. She asked for my help in telling her story. Now her story will live on for generations to come.

I WISH

I wish I was five again, and I could feel my mother's loving hands. I wish I was ten and hear her yell, "it's time to come in!"

I wish I would have known the hour she would pass, and we would part and then I would have lingered at dinner and talked until dark.

I would have been more patient with her stories and listened more carefully to what she said

I wish I was five and hiding under her bed

I wish I could hear her fake laugh at my jokes

And see her smile even when we played in the house, and things got broke

If I had known the hour that she would pass
and we would part, I would have skipped work
and taken her to the park.

For one last walk and one last long, meaningful
talk. I wish we could take another trip just she
and I

And we would talk and laugh and eat our
favorite sweet potato pie. I wish we could sit and
figure things out, just her and me

I wish I was five or maybe even three bouncing
happily upon her knee.

I wish I could feel her hands and kiss her face
and watch the hands of time rewind

and I could be nine with Mom in front and me
not far behind.

Oh, what I would give to be ten and me and Mom
could be forever friends again.

ABOUT THE AUTHOR

Diane Johnson is a recent retiree of the Defense Finance and Accounting Service Columbus, Ohio where she served 30 years in many positions to include; supervisor, branch chief, division chief and training and procedures specialist. She has many talents and now has time to explore her gifts and express her creative nature. She has always enjoyed writing poetry, song lyrics and short stories.

Diane graduated from Marion-Franklin high school in 1977 and went on to graduate from the Ohio State University in 1982 with a Bachelors of Arts in communication. She also went on to pursue a Masters of Arts from Central Michigan University in 2010. With a thirst for knowledge Diane has also achieved certification as a grantwriter, paralegal and notary public.

She is devoted to her loving husband James Salter, and spending time with family is very important to her. She enjoys reading the word of God, daily mediation, and helping others through her non-profit organization "Seeds of Faith."

Home | Seeds of Faith (seedsoffaithcorp.com)